The Scorpion's Mineral Eye

The Scorpion's Mineral Eye

J. Medina

SD
CWP

SAN DIEGO
CITY WORKS
PRESS

ISBN 978-0-9816020-2-8
Library of Congress Control Number: 2018946465

San Diego City Works Press is a non-profit press, funded by local writers and friends of the arts, committed to the publication of fiction, poetry, creative nonfiction, and art by members of the San Diego City College community and the community at large. For more about San Diego City Works Press please visit our website at www.cityworkspress.org.

San Diego City Works Press is extremely indebted to the American Federation of Teachers, Local 1931, without whose generous contribution and commitment to the arts this book would not be possible.

Cover design: Rondi Vasquez
Production editor: Will Dalrymple | Layout & Editing | willdalrymple.com

Published in the United States by San Diego City Works Press, California
Printed in the United States of America

To Margot, Chatas, and Migs

Contents

I. The Scorpion's Mineral Eye

II. The Sun-Splashed East San Diego Afternoon

III. Cauhtemoc: I Came Here to Find My Heritage

I.

The Scorpion's Mineral Eye

From the Land of Scorpions

30–30 rifles blast into the morning twilight.
Mom's friends pull triggers, fire into Orion.
A Norteno group sings, "La Golandrinas."
"A donde iras . . . la golandrina de aqui te vas."
This song sends us with Ave Maria's
Into the Sierra Madre. We head for El Norte.

This ranch does not produce beans or corn.
Gone is the precious silver and pine forests.
They have been stolen by gabacho corporations:
"Grupos," "Sindicatos," and "Companies."
Tarahumaras have fought the good fight.
Now, many are long gone, hung from broken branches,
Had shootouts, or have left for El Norte.
This ranch now only produces narco ballads.

I crouch near the creek, the inner curve
Of my youth. I see a reflection of a dove.
The dove too flies beyond its coo.
"O cielo santo . . . adios, adios."
Dip my hand into the holy water,
Make the sign of the cross,
Kiss the bronze soil.

The Sierra Madre's breath guides us
Past boulders, deer, wild boars.
Scorpions lurk everywhere. This is their land.
Their mineral eyes stare, perched for attack.
Another creek, I squat at the water's edge:
The morning crescent moon
Comes through the pine cones.
There is no trail. I look ahead: Nothing
But the unkown, spine forest future

I hold my skull. I remember leaping free,
Beyond my youth's breath, mounting my mare
galloping into the mouth of my ranch.
"Junto a mi pecho, hallaras su cielo."
All I know now is that my cielito lindo
Has been snuffed by my starving belly.
We lead our burros, our mules
Past shoulders of ridges, past hillsides.
Down we go past mountain hips.

Stop! I shape a mountain into a new heaven.
Beyond the landscape, a new valley,
A new Durango. We pull down a new moon.
Here a star catches a peso.

Tomorrow, I will see signs that scream Coca-Cola.
I will not know why a General Motors car
Stops at a stoplight, why saxophone music
Comes out of a box with knobs,
Or why lips make a weird shape
To utter incomprehensible sounds.
"O cielito lindo, adios."

My Tongue Made a Weird Shape

We arrived in San Diego.
I did not know a word of English.
The transistor played:
A dj said something about vacations.
Listening became my divine, inherent vice:
My teacher said that's how I would learn.

Over the summer, I uttered English words.
My tongue careened, tripped,
slipped, crashed into my mouth's wall;
in the distance, the sound of the bough
Broke in a gentle wind.
I was deaf to the breath in words.
The waves did not come to the shore.
In my throat, the lungs' wind became lost.
My skin stretched; my veins swelled.

I turned to the song of birds,
To the wind's music.
New sounds formed in my throat.
Fresh water verbs mouthing
Its stream into our creek.

I lip-synched to Motown, Dylan, and Hank.
I wanted to sing their poetry.
My lips quivered, trembled.
When I repeated the words,
I was scared, haunted
By the unknown vocabulary,
Not by the meaning,
but by mysterious, English foreign sounds.
Those words ricocheted
Back with a pang into my mouth.

In school, I remained silent.
I cowered, shrunk into my desk.
The teacher called on me.
Cynthia and Terry snickered
At my bruised consonants:
Share/chair, shine/chin.
Ralphie and Mike said, "Don't worry!"
I lost sleep.
I could not think of my message.
A butterfly lost in sun's flight.
I suppressed a lip moan.
I saw the pulled jaw of others
Laugh, mimic, snicker at my pronunciation.
My syllables shook with a fractured terror.
I spoke only with nods, with eyes,
With my arms and shoulders.

Now, if I am anywhere,
I still want to sing,
"Volver y Volver" and "El Rey,"
I don't want my mother tongue
Cut in half, smashed to the bottom teeth.
I want my two tongues in my mouth.
A golandrina looks for its nest.

Angela Before an Earthquake

In a marketplace
in Tijuana, blue flies
buzz on splattered papayas.
Angela blinks, glances
at the marketplace
and does not notice
the wind, motionless.
Around tree branches,
dogs smell each other.
She did not see
that the birds are gone.
Angela pulls her head
back into the kitchen,
pierces the lonely eye
of a fish
gutted in the sink.
Her eyes dart again
to the marketplace;
they trace the flight
of a dragonfly.
The tiny veins
on its shadowed wings
fall on a stranger.
In the shade
his white teeth sink
through the skin of guava.
Angela wraps the fish
in smoked leaves.
Tomorrow, she thinks
sweeping across the tile floor,
tomorrow, I will dress for him.
She presses lace
against her dark nipples.
Outside Angela's window,

beyond the acacias,
feint tremors ruffle dead leaves.
The musical chimes
quiver in stillness, stillness.

Undoing Frida's Retrato de Mi

Nerve slacks in the middle spine
Guitarviolindreamstrings royaltrumpetcall
Tierrabronze azulcantina mariachimusic
"Cu ru ruuu, ru cuuu paloma."
In Frida Khalo's *Retrato de Mi*
Scissors unwind lavendersky
A monolith rises tothedarksky
Meteorflash falls ingreensky
Tangerinespots a wall longbronzelegs
Tequila bienborracho suspendedonhangingcocks maroonbras
I trace the flightof adragonfly
Transparentwing falls
On a half opendoor otramujermexicana
She sits nearasun flower
A redrose fragrancefalls intopanpussydulce
A yellowhibiscus inoneear shesings
"La Llorona" sneaks me to La Maliche
Another mujer's legs hang froma jacaranda
Warmwind lifts herminiskirt a jasminesmell
Golandrinas Pedro Infante suavevoice deamantes
Legs now shakeabranch
Rubitsthighs a walkin lightwood
Davis's trumpet makes adoublecall
A monarcaunfoldingitsleftwing
Her wavy hair holding my breath
Until from nowhere Pancho Villa arrivesagain
NowAy, ay aaay's lift her to the pyramids
The world is alive on this canvas
what I imagined
Before I hadnotseen
A dance inFrida's fine painting ofme.

His Arms Are His Everyday Wings

Off Second Avenue,
In Tijuana, I see
On a mechanic's trolley
A legless man.
With a guitar
He sits so still,
So mute, unmindful
As though unborn.

Girls come out
Of a fashion store.
He watches them
Shake their braids.
In a light so young,
So old, he handles
His guitar so gently.
I feel the sad note
Break in his mouth
When he sings Pedro Infante's
"La Golandrina." He has soft hair,
grave, sweet dark eyes.
As I look at him,
He stretches out
On the curb
And sleeps.
He dreams of the day
When his bones
Will be carried away.
He awakens, places
His hand on his kidney,
Looks up and is scared
By the boots of a woman
Approaching between trees.
He pushes himself

Out of her way.
His lips ask for the Virgin of Guadalupe.

The hand on my arm
Fears to feel
My own wing blade,
And I shudder to think
That he will never leave
Footprints on a beach
Because his legs
Have been turned to dust.

My Monarca Wings Around My Margot

I fly from my Michoacan fir
to El Norte
pastthepoisonwind
into intoxicating liquor of pollen
when I rest   kissmymilkweed   I fold
my wings   mount   my monarca   for passionseconds
clouds pass us by
sleepy plants awaken
wet cinnamon soilfragrance
mockingbird sings meteor through sky
her legs wrap around my breath
we laugh, splash sun separates us
Female sexscent
remainon my wings
I fly away   Dance in flight
Leap lavender seaflowers
Hurricanthunderblownoise   knocks me down
A man approaches   on a bike
Sun   shinesthrough   a   parted cloud
Hetouches   blowswarmbreath   my   deadwing

Somewhere along this san diego barrio   he thinks
This monarca in its path
Will end happy here
He leaves me
In a rose bed

II.

The Sun-Splashed East San Diego Afternoon

Say Hey

Once I caught a ball like you, Willie Mays.
I made my hands, arms into a basket.
You were so 24. You did it with such grace.
I thought I saw all summer in your gaze.
Wherever you are "Say Hey," you are not gone;
You remain in my memory when I chase
After the white ball falling from the moon, my legs
Running beyond the sound of my own breath.
One night, I lost the ball for an instant
In the lights. When I looked up, the ball brushed
My glove's web. I cursed, swung my flailing arm
And chased the ball clear out to the far fence.
That would not happen to you. Running under
The ball, your gold glove was a living cupped hand.
You were made for roaming out there in centerfield,
Catching the world like wind, when the glare disappears.

Loss of Innocence

Esperanza has learned to survive.
Throughout the years, she recites novenas,
Lights votive candles.
The light swells to its arc.
Still she hears the flag draped coffin of her Tomas
Lowered into the darkness.

His rocking chair sways empty.
Esperanza calls out to her Tomas
in half breath,
"Chato, ven pa' aca, abrazame."
She calls out to him
In the innocent first love voice.
Esperanza wonders if he hears her—
Her mouth dried open
In its calm prayer.

That afternoon in the San Diego Navy Hospital,
Doctors allowed her to stay,
To watch her Tomas sleep forever,
To look at the blood remains
Near his black orchid temple.
Tomas decided, "Ya, chale con esto."
Shot the pain out of his skull.

Esperanza half expected his body to flinch,
An eyebrow to twitch, a lip nerve to say, "Ay, mi vida!"
Or to hear the pain groan
Rise from the corner of his heart,
Maybe, maybe even hear her name,
"Esperanza, Esperanza!"
Anything she could hang on to now,
Rather than the sob empty heart drain of his numbness.

Sometime near two pm,
She left her Tomas.
She could not get the war out of her:
Why her Tomas enlisted to kill,
Why the Cong looked to kill him,
How he inhaled an orange strange air,
Saw eyes dangling from branch trees.
Tomas could not sleep without the skull scream.

That afternoon, out of breath from sobbing
The sky turned bone grey.
Underneath his picture
Next to the Virgin, I left candles,
Heard his voice lost in the dark turning light.

Innocence Gone Awry

"Let the world go forth
from this time and place
...that the torch
has been passed
to a new generation
of Americans...."
JFK

You tried to lift
Your golden head
With your marvelous strength,
But it was no use.

That sun-splashed
East San Diego afternoon:
School let out.
I strapped myself to a silver pole—
Closer to heaven to see you.
Wind blew your shining hair.
Your eyes, envisioned a new frontier—
The nation, unequal before,

Now in search for King's Dream,
In search of new moon.
Now the tongue of a branch is broken.
That afternoon
I walked past the trees,
Past the stucco suburbia,
Stepped through our door.
My mother knelt, prayed
In front of La Virgin Guadalupe.
"Asesinaron al Presidente.
No quiero verlo asi!"
Her hair fell over wet cheeks.

Full of swollen tangled tears,
My Jefa cried the rest of the afternoon.

Now, mi Presidente,
You lay in your tomb
With your hands open,
With your eyes open,
Seeing this purgatorial nation,
Lost in its own fear, moral corruption,
Hidden in the mind light
Of a broken, despaired heart,
Rubbing its hands on the temple of cynicism.
Gone is "...for one fleeting moment
That was known as Camelot."

Mi Presidente, I want to be
The torch, the arch
Of the votive flame—
The breath of a new frontier.

Ball's Bullet Echo

For Nick, Reuben, and Ted

The racquetball shot misses its mark.
I want that shot back.
Someone once said,
We don't get second chances,
But in any game, heaven's stars reappear.
With light in his arms—my brother places the ace.
Our racquets clang in celebration.

Mercury glides past the hill's long grass
Passes wildflowers, picks these flowers
Hands them to women in open skirts;
Their legs touched by his wind.

I want to glide like Mercury,
Be touched by the wind—
This game drives my time.
I hop into the held hope
Of youth's garden.

Before I enter the court,
I hear the ball's bullet echo
In dream's dark corner.
I chase the ball, quickness of hand,
Cut the cunning angle,
Hit the ball with all my heart.
Sometimes, I hit Nick,
Leave blue welts,
The sudden pain, a fire to the stars.
I rearrange my shoe's tongue.
My skull breathes, lets in new air.

I imagine Aztec warriors:
They bang their shields,

Pound their chests,
Chant: “oooh, oooh, woahooo.”
They cup their hips like grasshoppers,
Use their flanks to pass the ball
Through the baked red clay circled “O.”
They chant: “oooh, oooh, woahoo.”

Now, I smell my sweat;
Flick it at the scarred wall.
I want my glory Aztec held shield
To place the ball beyond others’ breath,
But my nephew measures the distance,
Smacks the ball past me into the void.

I stand unknowing of my lost position.
In another breath’s serve,
I return his golden shot
Into the freezing darkness of the corner—
I am the flowered chalice of a new air.

Undash the Dash Man

I look down the lane.
My breaths come furiously.
The hiccup, belch, stumbles
Into the bottom of barf.

"Set!" yells the starter.
Guns have blasted before.
This will thunder in 2.5 seconds.
I dig my spikes into the blocks.
My veins are filled with blood.
Temples sweat, vibrate anxiety.
My inner voice tells me:
Take a deep breath, slack the nerve.
That is the way with us dash men:
Try to beat my all-time best.

We break out of the blocks—
Undergo the floodlight of moon, tangerine sun.
I do not notice the cinnamon sky,
The mechanical sound of jets
Or the cars on the Five South.

Nor do I hear the animals,
The birds in the nearby SD Zoo.
I do not notice the still breeze.
I do not hear the screams from the Navy Hospital,
Or the orgasmic sound of fans.
I only hear the still beat of my heart,
The scissors silent cut of the rose stem.
I only feel the wind's thrust.
Feel the rush of the exhaled breath.

Some legs move quietly, faster than mine.
I lean into the curve.

I pass some shoulders.
Arms, hips pass me on the straightaway.
We go into the final turn.
Spikes push Mercury's wing on tartan.
A trumpet's call parcels the last sixty yards.
The kick of the brilliant heart nears the tape,
One last benzedrine breath brain push—
Now, I lean forward to the king light of victory.

Flaco

The last time I saw Flaco,
He walked down the avenue.
One leg moved faster than the other.
His prosthesis arm, still in a sling.
The other arm veined all over.
His hair thinner than air.
Flaco stared right past me.

Putas know his name;
They open their hips to him.
Flaco listens to their numb greetings—
To him this sounds like the mechanical wave,
Engines that match the thunder
Of artillery trucks he drove in Nam.
He remembers: I drove past the nipa leaves,
Past the wet rice fields.
Above us, the helicopters sprayed fire;
Further ahead, jets dropped shrapnel bombs.
I drove past fingers without direction,
Past a pumping liver.

La vida vale madre, he says to himself.
Eyes burnt into sockets is what I saw.
We dodged land mines.
A rocket shell hit my engine.
The shrapnel tore my carnal's
Left shoulder to dust.
Only bougainvillea blood remained.
The rest of the shrapnel tore skin.
We awoke in morphine tents.
Now Flaco stops at the corner light.
The mannequins at the store
Stare at him and wink.
"Hey, Flaco," a lady calls,
"Hey, Flaco, need help?"

The Thrilla

The fight starts quickly, a medium pace;
soon bad Muhammed will work on his face.
Muhammed shuffles and glides to the side,
This rubber match: the gold arc of light pride.
Frazier throws left hooks, works tough underneath,
The shots jar ribs, then tries to rearrange teeth.
With Frazier half staggered and partially blind,
Muhammed knows that Frazier is way behind.
Muhammed carries Mercury's winged feet;
If not, he will be in the third-row seat.
Poor Frazier is done; he prays to the sky,
But none of the praying will open his eye.
Frazier's corner throws in the towel: gone!
The Greatest has outfought death—he is done.

Too Long in One Place

Sandra wears white pants,
A faded yellow blouse
That nearly matches
The restaurant's faded tablecloths.
Her eyes, amber, filled with fire,
Dart to a clock, then in a swirl
Just sits and aimlessly stares
Like a life-term prisoner at the floor.

She wants to split this part-time job;
She has picked up countless times,
Gone to train, bus stations,
Airports, hitchhiked past the tumbleweeds,
Past the lost, windswept dreams.
Sat next to people who swapped stories
Of what could have been,
Only to want more, a new heaven.
Sandra has a degree in English
Once taught in a Guadalajara school,
Was a freeway, bygone flyer.
One Thursday afternoon,
After getting paid,
She wrote across the blackboard,
"I have gone fishin'—Dig you later!"
But really wanted to write,
Fuck all this kiss-ass life.

In fifteen months, she returned, broke.
Now, in a dim, effervescent pizza joint,
Smoking one cigarette after another,
Swallowing coffee, swallowing regrets,
Wishing she worked in the empire of the bitch-goddess,
Not in stockyards, chicken slaughterhouses,
Not for pimps who use Nikons on her naked flesh,

Or staying bleary-eyed awake
On meth to dangle legs on yesterday's poles,
Or to leave dream drama romances.
Now she feels the tightness of her hair bun.
Touches loose strands that tangle themselves
on her heart-shaped earrings.
Sandra places her cup on the table,
Sits in silence, a fragmented universe,
Inhales more smoke, shrugs.

Her left side of the shoulder,
Tilts her eyes toward a midday light.
Sandra heads for the doorway.

Keep on Peddlin'

For Mike Sinyard

A gentle morning lake breeze
Slices through last night's water,
Through branches, bush,
And the eternal Miles's trumpet.
I am in the saddle of my bike.
Cool air enters my skull.

I ride my bike past an awakened buck moon.
Mothers push baby strollers:
God's wonders tucked in breath's new heaven.
Nowadays, spandex makes me curious;
Its fabric upholds the upside-down heart.
Shaped hips dissolve into clouds.
My bike holds the morning curve.
I lean sideways.
Birds in branches raise their church song.
Another heron: still, quiet as crested water.
The osprey: its gold eyes
Overlooks its kingdom
Remaining closer to heaven than the rest of us.

Keep peddlin'
I stare at a dirt field.
Wind raises a powder dust.
I slow down.
I imagine our soldiers in Iraq awake at night,
Listening to their own breath.
Now, a missile miles away, shakes the desert.
The soldiers hold their rifles closer,
Ready to point and blast ISIS
Twilight's meteor into dust.

A short straightaway on the road.
I pick up the pace.
Now, I imagine I am on a fast break.
I am on the wing.
Pistol Pete's pass is shoveled to me.
It's three on two.
I dribble guardlike for three steps—
Stay in my lane;
Sidehand, pass the orange back to Pistol Pete.
The ball moves to the other wing.
My man Bird takes the ball to the air,
Kisses it off the glass, into the dream gossamer.

Now, I coast down an incline.
"Ay, ay, ayyay, canta y no llores,
porque cantando se alegran cielito lindo los corazones."
In a shadow of an instant
my Cantinflas self passes me
then reappears in tamarind light.

I keep on peddlin'.
I pass a woman on her walk.
Her wide brim hat
Keeps the sun's ray away.
Under her skin is the real light.
Neruda, not far away,
Holds his fishing line
Waiting for the perfect poet's line.
Another straightaway—a speed burst:
"Miami, Florida; Atlanta, Georgia;
Raleigh, North Carolina, Night Train, Night Train."
Churn the blood—fill, Godfather of Soul, the heart!

Now, my ride comes to an end;
Flick my sweat away.
My breath comes in short spurts.
The lake's water edge sings
To a budding wild flower.

III.
Cauhtemoc: I Came Here to Find My Heritage

An Unsent Letter to Heaven's Address

There are no regrets.
Only this idea: If we could have had more time,
We could have done a million things.
Esta vida sin ti esta loca.
I write this letter to you, Margot:
To breathe life into your picture.
I will not put it out for the postman.
I walk to the window,
Coil my fingers in the frame,
Gaze absently across the blur,
Feel the golpe sin amor.
Know that I am the absence
Of this space in the vacant living room.
Even as I stand here, blurred memories,
Breathe an unknown sigh,
Que onda con esta locura?
I walk aimlessly,
A baile triste without direction.
With tequila in hand,
I make a circle
Stop and in the middle of this afternoon.

Shadows throw themselves
Long in the hardwood.
This letter will not be answered.
I remember the time when I cradled
Myself in your thighs, Margot.
I sang, "Tu y Solamente Tu."
Danced pansa a pansa.
I hugged you like a ripe mango,
Felt the wind in the hills,
Touched the gurgle in the brook.
And because I am your husband, lover,
I will be your Pedro Infante in heaven.

Bright sunflowers,
Jade, and rancheras pa' tu corazon.
I miss your big round brown eyes,
Your juicy jamaica-red lips,
Your graceful long arms around me.
Now, all I have is the dream of you.
In the quiet of this breath,
I hold tight to this letter
I accept as life.

Sleep Walk in Sancho's Windmills

I have come to appreciate this suave viento.
Now that I am in the light side of 60,
this element grooms my hair,
allows jacarandas, roses to enter my skull,
embrace me like un viejo amigo.
Halfway currents caught in jasmine,
sleepwalk in Sancho's windmills.
In Miles's trumpet, tigers jump out of their eyes,
in Dylan's wind it blows *Howl.*
This wind picks up leaves,
throws them against a fence,
with the same breath
as the one in my single heartbeat.
Now the wind swings the gate
past lost memories,
into scattered long shadows of afternoons.
I move my hand, move the wind,
Wind breaks into cup cheeks,
Into the lusty coos of palomas,
Into cars where young lovers
kiss each other's own breath
toss the world's intimacies of middle sex.
Now the wind rushes into tall trees, then with a fury to llanos.
This suave viento has blown like this all the time;
Yet I have not remembered it so.

Juicy as Drunk Mango

I go to her in the midnight air.
My mouth juicy as a drunk mango.
My lover is naked and knowing my wish
has kept only the regalia of her jewelry.
I stand firmly in her middle.
Coos of doves, wind shake leaves,
water gurgles in streams.
Her eyes open, naked as stars.
From the quiet of her waist
her long legs lead to her body of water.
I lick the pollen between her thighs.

Wheeled Out

I am wheeled out of the operating room.
My neck slumped, looks broken.
Staring down at the waxed floor,
Skinny shafts of light reflect
Pillow-pressed patients' muttered breaths;
Others' eyes hide heaven's numbness;
Others' hands in a knot, float in uncertainty.

Now, I limp in flame-fury pain.
A branch breaks in the wind.
One leg moves faster than the other.
I prop myself up.
Ice my water-filled knee,
Bring the cloud down.

Now anesthesia runs through my veins,
Lodges itself, whirls, smacks into a numb muscle.
Broken glass grinds through dog-day knee,
Shakes my thin breath.
I need another pill now, "lla pues!"
Take me deeper into wound sleep.
A mustang shakes its mane,
its anxious eyes ready to gallop.
A giggling black woman,
Black olives in a silk red bra.
Her thighs hold mariposas. Twenty mile stretches from San Diego to Tucson,
Blowing memory's unlocked marijuana,
The heavenly, harmony music of Los Lonely Boys.

The dryness of my mouth,
The smell of my piss,
Ripped lavender water awakens me;
Leaves swept by yesterday's wind,
Leave me floating. I want to walk.

One leg feels the floor,
The other is too drunk to take a step.
I used to run through water.

Mi Siesta

Morpheoustapsme on the lefttemple.
Wispy tangerineclouds unhinge dream.
The night isdarker than buried stones.
Wind's teal message rests on my Sierra Madre:
"Sal Si Puedes!"
Adragonfly's transparent wing
falls on cinnamonchi-chis,
Flies toballgrindingcock, orchid shaped pussy.
When I pass Gila Bend,
I toss aMexicanpeso over abridge.
Its rcflcction fallson yesterday'scoineyecows.
From a pictureless convalescent room
My mom screams intoareflection ofherskull,
prays Ave Marias to avoid
thelone memory ofshoulder.
I drink ojosmalaguenos another tequilashot.
Pirouette above thebasketballrim,
lookdown at thegossamer,
delivertheworld tothe sweetswishsound.
Breakthrough theracetape
throughthe sirensong light.

listen mariachis.
Carmenblows marijuana
toescurl towards crimsonnube.
I turn her ultimate pan dulce,
Place onehand onher mouthedstomach,
listen "Ay, Ay, Ay" hanginherbreath.
Her nervegoddess moves a Muddyblue guitar,
water overrocks, apricotleaves turn onsand.
Marvin singsto curvethe flesh.
Flanked by tamarindo,
In bronzelies hercielito lindo.
Abranch trembles,
palomasreturn from theirsiesta.

TokyJuana

Tela gets paid to dance.
Here, in this teal glass warehouse,
Japanese moons hang upside down.
Hieroglyphic banners swirl in jasmine air.
Banda horns drive hips.

Tela is a mujer in motion.
She rotates on a pole.
I watch her Mexican chocolate shoulder
Turn clouds into a sexual light curve.
Now, Tela turns her back to me,
Looks at me through her parted legs—
A splash of ocean water
A dove rests on her nest.
The half orange moon rises
Over Japanese maple trees.
Pink lips, geisha eyes, cheerleader bronze calves,
And now her raven hair comes undone.
I inhale the lotus.

Tela loves no hombre.
Man after man has thrown her
Away like an old mango peel.
She does not kiss any man on the lips,
Only pirouettes chichi and hip
to forget the hombre with the sombrero
Big belt buckle rape of innocence
Tela skirts the floor's edge.
Next to me dollars are tucked
Into Saturday's stars.
I place a five in her powerful silk spot.
My fingers unfurl a butterfly's wing wall.
The norteno song tells of Tela:
She is all bougainvillea and iron.

My Primitive Words

Margot, my words are primitive,
like the rain, like the sun.
When I say your name,
music coos like our palomas.
The words fall on your arms.
The words rest there,
As I rest in thighs' tenderness.
"Soy para ti,
tu eres para mi.
Tu sabes muy bien
Que te quiero, siempre."
Your fingers caress my hair.
I run mine through your curls.
I look at your marvelous eyebrows,
Your red lips, roses in my garden.
I call out your name in dream... Margot, Margot.

Cloudtuckedmoonflower

Sindi's only wish istolive likeripefruit
I sitnext to her
she looksohot inher redmini
eyes beyond words transfixed now hombres
openmouthed forget themselves
by looking hornyhuman at her
she carries therush ofmethfloodblood
human corrido tapsherfinger topass dullgreytime
ahalflaugh the soundofbluepesetas alostheart
numbtoamor hardcoverslips unable tokiss
undresses pain leavesmisery in her past
leaves hombres exhalingthrobbing
waftsofsmoke hallucinating neonlights
Sindi dancevibrates herhips a garden intoxicatinglightrhythmmujer
Makes manballs want her mujerhood
Herperfume cloudtuckedmoonflower
Hertamarindomayanbronzeskin sensetripdream
shesipsoncheapgin
Sindimonarcawants toflyout ofherblouse rosebudcaresseschichi
Eveningjasmine betweenherthighs
Sindi has abigbeltsombrerohombre
Follow hercorazon'scoldblood toan
emptycloud turnedupsidedownredmoonflower

The Zephyr Underneath the Wild Parrots

Somewhere in this world of mine.
I see people squeeze each other.
I see mountains and lakes
Hold tight earth's air.
In my backyard, wild parrots fly through velvet air.
They head for another home.

Wherever you are, Margot, close or distant,
The sound of parrot wings
Exhales the same sound as your wings.
The wings breath announces
the entrance or the departure
from God's light kingdom.
I feel your presence in these
Familiar surroundings
The sun warms my heart
Later, crystal drops of rain
Bless my forehead.
After the drizzle, clouds shape a "Chata" face.
No matter, I am wrapped in gentle music of parrot wings.

The Middle of My Mariachi

I look at a rose in its vase,
listen to inner heart of violin strings.
Air currents carry wishes
of love's passion desires.
Now, a guitarron with wide sombrero
awakens Mexican ojos cafes,
pelo chino, lips with the taste of maguey.
Every lyric moves cold and hot, sun and moon.

The heart lets out its blood.
We leave Mexico; the song does not leave us.
The suave canto is the same:
"No tengo reina ni trono. . . ."
We may go to unkown lands
Yet we carry the nostalgic crown;
we are kings of our own domain.

To touch the cloud,
to find the golden oil,
to light the senses
and sing, "Y sigo siendo El Rey."

You Are Not Matt Anymore

"Fuck Your Ethnicity."
—Kendrick Lamar

Tia taps my shoulder.
Headphones cover my ears.
She taps again.
Points to the door.
"Yes, may I help you?"
"Are you Matt Macias?"
No need to nod.
From his shirt pocket,
The officer pulls an ICE badge.
A rose has died in the garden.
I kneel, pray.
I have done this a million times before.
This is the last time here.
"Hail Mary full of grace. . . ."
The Virgin will hear me.

"Pack your belongings. . . ."
I am unable to hear myself breathe.
Tia knows.
I hug her for the last time.
Our still hearts meet.
Tia gives me her blessings.
An angel kiss lands on my forehead.
Tia's tear-eyes dry mine.
I leave her, leave Rolando Bl.
On the 94W, my San Diego skyline,
Disappears into a flower sunset.
I disappear, afraid, into darkness.

A different tia now speaks.
"Mira, mira Mateo,
alla no quieren los Mexicanos.

Alla, Trump dice que eres un criminal."
Trump wants the death of DACA.
Dreams to Trump—now your nightmare.
Mateo, now meet Quetzalcoatl.
Forget the huddled masses of the Statue of Liberty.
Now, meet Frida and Diego,
Sunflowered branch-broken spine.
Listen, dance now to jarocho guitar.
Don't forget the language of Hemingway.
The gavachita… forget marrying her for citizenship.
She is Daisy: A Fitzgerald myth!
Mateo used to listen to Kendrick,
Whistles now "Cielito Lindo."
A shiny heaven lands sideways.
Whales return to their Baja.
Monarcas return to their fir.

His tia reminds Mateo,
"your skin color, all no vale.
Aquie somos la tierra."
Kendrick warned me:
Haters of color are in the land of the free.
Trump in his White House,
The corn-haired Trompa,
Fuquen nazi lover, the lyen fuquer.
I wanted to be a Marine, to build bridges:
God's oil created us all equal,
Gave us inalienable rights,
In ramparts yet wave.
A new moon sings me to a new dream.
A new sun's light awakens new skin.
Quiet air rushes through my temples.
Forget the American Dream—
Make Mexico now better.

Luna, Sol, Magic Runes

I pack a camera,
Travelers cheques.
Socks and shirts
Into my suitcase.
My brother drives me
To Tijuana's depot.
On the bus I read
Aztec Thought and Culture.
I fall asleep:
Two stones make a wall
Wind in my palm
A finger points
Toward a garden blue.
I'm awakened by crying
Children. An old woman
Next to me
Smells of babies.
I excuse myself
To see dragonflies
Splattered on the front window.
We cross Mil Cumbres, Popo.
In La Capital
Streets are cluttered
With tourists who breathe
Through small holes,
See through small holes.
Rain comes, slips
Drop by drop through ivy.
Hot wind! Too many doors
Open here,
And the faces of strangers
Belong to Franceses y Alemanes.
In La Catedral,
Women recite yesterday's novenas.

Their knees walk
On rough stones
For fifty yards,
And all they get
in return is blood.
I take a bus to Teotihuacan.
Moon, Sun, magic ruins
Carved in obsidian
Refined by water.
I stand on this volcanic rock
Drink pulque.

My footprints stamp solid
In La Avenida de los Muertos.
In the entrance
To the pyramid of the Sun
A serpent's tongue is gold.
I imagine the poet Nezahualcoyotl
Walking on gold, tangerine pebbles
Whispering in a garden to Quetzacoatl:
"What does your mind seek?
Where is your heart?
If you give your heart
To each and everything
You destroy your heart."

Warriors compare dings,
Their time worn shields.
Maxtla, the merchant,
boasts of quetzal feathers.
Xochitl laughs at the aqua fish
From the silver lake.
I go back to the City,
See the museum where water
Moves up a monolith,
To a place where the sky
Is still a question.
Cartolandia, where dogs,
Lie drunk, like banana peels.

I go to Chapultepec,
Cauhtemoc's house.
The November before the Spaniards
Burned his feet, he heard his master,
Huahuatzin chant:
"In the long night
I speak to dead remains
A winter's river is filled
With blood, open eyes face the moon;
We have lost the battle to the Gachupines."

In a plain altar, Cauhtemoc,
Women buried you well,
And for a benediction,
I pick a sunflower
Kneel, pray, lay it at your tomb.

That is why I came here—
To find myself in heritage,
To touch the past
Where rocks are like water
Stone set upon stone,
Where I may learn to sleep.

J. Medina, born in the Sierra Madre of Durango, Mexico and raised in San Diego, California, engages his norteño background, along with his Chicano roots, to forge his poems. The poet feels at home whether confronting a golf ball in the rough or expressing his views on banned books. As an English Professor at Grossmont College, he has been offering Reading and Composition classes for as long as the wind has been blowing. He enjoys his kids, his pugs, and his daydreams. "I want to stretch my emotional pendulum to develop images into lyrical lines that have yet to be imagined. I want to have readers ask, 'Y eso ques es?' " The chapbook's debut addresses his memories, his imagination, his loss of innocence, and his borracheras.